Mainak Dhar is a self-confessed cubicle dweller by day and a writer by night. After graduating from the Indian Institute of Management, Ahmedabad, he has spent more than fifteen years in the corporate world. At the same time, he has been a prolific writer, with ten books to his credit. Learn more about him and contact him at mainakdhar.com.

THE
CUBICLE
MANIFESTO

Change the Way You Work
and Reinvent Your Life

MAINAK DHAR

Vermilion
LONDON

1 3 5 7 9 10 8 6 4 2

Published in 2012 by Vermilion, an imprint of Ebury Publishing
First published in India by Random House India in 2012

Ebury Publishing is a Random House Group company

The Random House Group Limited Reg. No. 954009

Addresses for companies within the Random House Group can be found at
www.randomhouse.co.uk

A CIP catalogue record for this book is available from the British Library

The Random House Group Limited supports The Forest Stewardship
Council (FSC®), the leading international forest certification organisation.
Our books carrying the FSC label are printed on FSC® certified paper. FSC
is the only forest certification scheme endorsed by the leading environmental
organisations, including Greenpeace. Our paper procurement policy can be
found at www.randomhouse.co.uk/environment

Printed and bound by CPI Group (UK) Ltd, Croydon, CR0 4YY

ISBN 9780091947972

Copies are available at special rates for bulk orders. Contact the sales
development team on 020 7840 8487 for more information.

To buy books by your favourite authors and register for offers,
visit www.randomhouse.co.uk

Contents

As always,
for Puja and Aadi

Cubicle dwellers of the world unite.
You have nothing to lose but the
tyranny of your cubicles.

A Note to Fellow Cubicle Dwellers

How many hours a day do you cubicle?

No, you did not hear that wrong and, no, you should not start worrying about picking up a book whose first line seems to be a murder of the English language. Hidden in my question is a proposal. A proposal that we officially recognize the important role the office workstation plays in so many of our lives by elevating its status to that of a verb. In 2006, 'google' was officially recognized as a verb in the *Oxford English Dictionary*. Given that we spend so much more time sitting in cubicles or tucked behind partitions in open-plan offices than on any search engine, it seems only appropriate to officially recognize what it is that we do there. Here is my attempt at explaining what it means 'to cubicle':

The act of sitting in a confined workspace for extended hours, stifling interpersonal communication, creativity and any other expression of individuality, which makes the individual forget life beyond the immediate demands of the job.

Ring a bell? If it does, you can at least take heart from the fact that you are not alone. It is estimated that close to twenty million people in the United States alone work in cubicles, and the total value of the cubicle-making industry may be as high as three billion dollars.

How did this soul-killing invention come to be such an indispensable part of our daily lives?

The cubicle began with the best of intentions. It was invented by Robert Propst in the 1960s as a means to enhance productivity by allowing an executive to have all relevant information readily spread out in front of him or her. Years of cost cutting, the desire to cram as many people as possible in one area and lack of imaginative design by corporations has reduced this vision to the long columns of drab, restricted cubes that dissect the floorplans of many corporate offices today. Before he died, Propst is said to have lamented his contribution to 'monolithic insanity'.

Over time, the humble cubicle has come to be reviled and ridiculed as an object of scorn, and comic strips like *Dilbert* and movies such as *Office Space* have sought to portray the often bizarre side of modern corporate life that the cubicle sometimes symbolizes – a tool that enforces conformity and boredom in offices.

Many of you may not work in a classic cubicle, having instead partitions or your desk boxing you in.

It's the same deal: your working life is spent in a small, confined space.

Tempting as it might be, my intention is not to join the chorus of voices mocking the absurdity of cubicle dwelling. The first reason is a pragmatic one – being yet another addition to an already long list of similar books on the same theme is usually a sure ticket to literary obscurity. The second reason is a more philosophical one.

Corporations are also waking up to the fact that they have perhaps pushed things to an extreme and many of them are pioneering interventions like flexible work hours and seating. However, the reality for the bulk of cubicle or other 'pod' dwellers is not likely to radically change unless we also contribute to this change. Whether we like it or not, many of us will have to keep 'cubicling' (another word for the dictionaries to consider) for several years yet. The reason for this is simply an economic one – working helps pay the bills and gets us the lifestyle we desire. For others, it is also about feeling a sense of achievement and progression in life.

I firmly believe that if one doesn't like something, the only available courses of action are to fix it, accept it or get out of the way. Bitching never solves anything. Since most of us are not going to say goodbye to our partitioned workspaces soon, and I see no reason to meekly accept unpleasantness every day, this book is an attempt to show

how we can bring more joy into the time we spend there. And instead of thinking of ourselves as passive victims, how each and every one of us can take charge and change the way we cubicle for the better.

My intention behind writing this book is twofold. First, I hope it gets you thinking about how you approach work (and life) as you cubicle. If even one of the ideas presented in this fable strikes a chord, then I would consider my effort a success. The second objective is a simple one – to engage and entertain. We always learn better when we are having fun. So this book imparts its lessons in a way that, I hope, will make you smile.

Now, to the most important question. Why should you read a book on this subject written by me? I do not have a PhD in organizational behaviour, but perhaps I have the most important qualification of all.

I am one of you.

While I may not be able to conjure up a huge rally to support you, I am here, through the pages of this book, to stand by you as we confront the spectre of Cubicle Tyranny. Don't worry, I will not ask you to leave your job. This will be a revolution where, far from risking facing a firing squad, you may well enjoy yourself. The irony of it will be that, at the end of it all, you may find that overthrowing Cubicle Tyranny in fact helps liberate you to perform better at your job. Let me also reassure you that this 'revolution' does not encourage you to tear down your office or put your bosses on trial. The reality is that many of us need to work, not just out of economic necessity, but also to feel a sense of achievement and to use and sharpen our skills. The beauty of this 'revolution' is that it does not even require you to leave your workspace, let alone your job. It is simply a sum of the things you can do differently each day to cast off the tyranny of pressure and stress that so many of us take for granted in our tiny work areas, and free us to not just enjoy greater overall happiness, but also enjoy our work more. No matter what kind of organization you work in, or if you are a new hire or a senior manager, you will agree with one general truth – we do better in any activity when we are enjoying it, be it playing a game, performing on stage, making love or, indeed, working in a confined space.

What can just the two of us achieve? In my book, two is all it takes to start a revolution. Read on and we may yet succeed. And, yes, together we may even succeed in bringing a smile to Mr Propst's face, in that great cubicle in the sky.

Mainak Dhar

MAXIM ONE

THE SPECTRE OF CUBICLE TYRANNY

'I have sworn upon the altar of God, eternal hostility against every form of tyranny over the mind of man.'

THOMAS JEFFERSON

'Will you be coming home for dinner?'

Mayukh read the text message from his wife and sighed. Behind this simple question, there was another, more daunting one. The one he dreaded answering.

'Should we have dinner without you, *again*?'

He glanced at his watch. It was already seven in the evening and he still had the presentation to work on. His Managing Director would not be too happy if it wasn't ready for the big meeting the following week. Dinner with the family was something that could only happen in his imagination. There was no way he was going to get home on time. *Again*. As he pressed 'Send' on his mobile phone to let his wife know that he would be late, Mayukh remembered the last argument they had, when she had told him that he never seemed to have time for her or their son any more. He had explained that with a promotion coming up, and with a tough year forecast for the business, there was no way he could slacken at work. He was now Group Manager of marketing for consumer electronics at the top multinational Dynamix and was expected not only to do his share, but also lead by example.

Mayukh felt a dull headache come over him and wished his wife would realize that he was, after all, working this hard only for her and their future together. He glanced around at the neighbouring cubicles and saw his three direct reports hard at work as well. He took another sip of his Diet Coke and then got back to his laptop, eager to get the PowerPoint slides finished as fast as possible. The presentation had already been through three revisions with his boss and he knew that before the week was over there would be many more to come, which meant many more late nights. He wished that his wife, Sudha, would understand that he didn't enjoy staying late at the office, and that he, too, would love to be with his family, tucking into a hot, home-cooked meal.

Mayukh had always been very meticulous, the result of an upbringing that had emphasized academic excellence as being the only way to get ahead. He brought that same attitude to work, and wrestled with any problem till he got to a near-perfect, if not perfect, solution. However, the latest project that he was working on was taxing his normally high level of patience. He got up to fetch his fourth Diet Coke of the day – the regular source of caffeine that sustained his long work hours – when a beep alerted him to a new email. He inwardly groaned at the thought of another message from his boss.

4

There was a single message. And it wasn't his boss. It read, 'Important Employee Announcement. Please open now.' Another HR update, thought Mayukh. He opened the mail to see a single attachment entitled 'Announcements.doc'. Ah, promotions and layoffs, he thought. His curiosity was piqued and he quickly opened the attachment. His screen turned white, and a single line appeared in black in the centre of his screen.

The spectre of Cubicle Tyranny is haunting you

Panic swelled within Mayukh, as he realized that he may have just opened a virus-ridden file. 'Dear God, dear God, dear God,' he muttered, as he quickly pressed several keys, hoping to make the message disappear. Instead, the single line of black text just stayed there.

He popped his head above his cubicle and asked one of his colleagues if they had opened the email from HR, but was met with a blank look. Mentally kicking himself for having opened what had obviously been a spam email, he tried to switch off his laptop, but found that even that did not work. Frustrated and more than a little annoyed, he took out the battery from his laptop and when the irritating and mystifying message disappeared, he powered up his laptop again.

The screen flickered to life, but horror of horrors, the blank white screen was still there. This time, with another line of text. It read:

Welcome to
the Cubicle
Manifesto

Mayukh furiously banged at the keys, but to no avail. Finally in exasperation, he yanked the battery out again and packed up for the day. He spent the drive home fuming about the work he might have lost and hoping that the IT guys would be able to both recover his data and get rid of the virus that seemed to have infected his laptop.

He reached home just before eight, and a surprised Sudha opened the door. His three-year-old son, Aadi, ran up to him and hugged his leg, happy, for a change, to be able to see his father before he was sent to bed.

Mayukh did not notice the smiles on their faces, and sat wordlessly through dinner, worrying about his laptop. When they were in their bedroom, he whipped out his BlackBerry to write an email to the IT department, so that they would be on the job first thing in the morning. Sudha was about to ask Mayukh something, but seeing him immersed in his BlackBerry, she turned on her side and went off to sleep.

The IT guy repeated for the third time that there was nothing wrong with Mayukh's laptop, and that there was no sign of any virus. Also, all his data seemed to be intact. Mayukh wondered how that could be the case after what he had seen the previous night. However, he was relieved that he had not lost any of his work. He walked back to his cubicle and booted up his laptop. In seconds he was knee-deep in his PowerPoint presentation.

Between a couple of calls and his work, it was soon lunchtime. Knowing that he had some lost time from the previous night to make up, he quickly went to the cafeteria and grabbed a sandwich, planning to eat it in his cubicle while he worked. He opened Word and saw a single line on his screen.

*You are a slave
to your cubicle*

Mayukh thought he was going crazy. He tried to delete it but could not. In sheer exasperation, he banged his hand down on his desk with an expletive, making many of his colleagues look up from their screens. Now there was another message.

*Prisoners eat in
their cells. Free
men do not.*

He glanced at his uneaten sandwich and then again at the words on his screen. He had no idea what was happening, but the mumbo-jumbo seemed to strike a chord. He had always been so busy at work that he couldn't remember the last time he had had a decent lunch. Mayukh generally compromised lunch for something quick, which

8

would usually be eaten in meetings or, more likely, in his cubicle as he worked. He watched his team tentatively head for the door, glancing his way, hoping that he would not give them more work over lunchtime. Suddenly, Mayukh didn't want to eat his sandwich alone. On an impulse, he put it aside and walked up to them, asking them what their plan for lunch was. He could see the nervousness in their eyes, and wondered why they were so hesitant over such an innocent question. When they told him they planned to go to a Chinese restaurant next door, he asked if he could join them.

The initial hesitation soon melted away, and Mayukh found himself enjoying lunch. He found out that one of them was about to celebrate his anniversary in the coming month, and another was worried about his ageing father's health. Small details, but things he had never picked up sitting in his cubicle by himself. And so, for the first time in a long period, Mayukh had a decent meal for lunch, in the company of someone other than his laptop, and in surroundings a tad more comfortable than his cubicle.

Back at his cubicle, he spent the rest of the afternoon as he usually did – on calls with colleagues in other locations and reading the dozens of emails that he got every day. He saw two missed calls from his wife, and told himself that he would call her back when he got a free moment. He was looking at a memo that one of his colleagues had prepared when his Internet browser seemed to come up on its own. The page displayed on the screen was his wife's Facebook page. He was about to close it when the screen went white and a now familiar line of text appeared.

Even prisoners get time to call their family

Sheepishly, he picked up his phone and called Sudha, who seemed surprised to hear from him in the middle of an office day. She reminded him that he needed to go for his health checkup in two days and also that his son's school would have their open day in three days. Mayukh grunted in agreement; he had totally forgotten about the annual school event. But at the moment, he had a more pressing issue – his big presentation.

At half past five, he sent an email out to his team, telling them that they would need to meet at six for an urgent meeting. He had just received an email from his boss enquiring about Project Pocketbook. They were slightly behind the target that had been set for their product line, and Mayukh wanted to make sure that he had a proper analysis and estimate first thing in the morning. He peeked over his partition wall to see his team gathered together, and he could guess that they were moaning about yet another late night. When they saw him looking at them, they scattered back to their respective cubicles.

At six, his work was once again rudely interrupted when his screen turned white.

Even prisons have their lights-off time

And then his laptop shut off, seemingly of its own accord. Mayukh tried to reboot it, but failed. He walked over to the IT guys who booted it up in no time, and looked at Mayukh strangely, wondering why he kept coming back complaining about some fictional virus in his computer. Mayukh sheepishly went back to his cubicle but the moment he tried to open his email, the white screen was back, and with it another line.

If you can't be free of Cubicle Tyranny, don't imprison others

Then his laptop shut down again.

Mayukh could see his colleagues waiting for him. He cursed the strange virus that was getting in his way all the time. He was about to ask one of his team to get their laptop, when he paused. He remembered the words on the laptop screen, and then called his team. He told them that they could do the meeting first thing the next morning, and asked them to call it a day.

Mayukh had never seen his colleagues so surprised or so delighted. As they left the office, he too packed his bag and left for home. As soon as he stepped out of the office, Mayukh realized that it had been a very long time since he had left for home when there was still sunlight outside. He hated to admit it, but a part of him felt guilty for having left early. He had been so conditioned to his late nights at work that he felt lost away from the comforting drabness of his cubicle.

He wasn't exactly sure of what he could do with all the time he now had on his hands, so he called Sudha. She was shocked to hear that he was coming home, and even more pleasantly surprised when he suggested that they go to their favourite seafood restaurant for dinner. After all, it had been ages since they had been out to eat.

That evening, as they shelled crabs and spooned up wriggly bits of squid, Mayukh reminisced about all the things that he loved about Sudha and their relationship. He had been so caught up in work over the last couple of years that he didn't even remember when he had last sat down with her like this, just eating, talking and enjoying each other's company. He missed their time alone together.

Before sleeping, Mayukh glanced at his laptop bag, wondering what strange virus had afflicted his laptop and what other surprises it would bring the next day. Little did he know that the virus had set in motion a strange turn of events.

MAXIM TWO

A COMPANY CALLED YOU CORP

'To see what is in front of one's nose needs a constant struggle.'

GEORGE ORWELL

When Mayukh walked into his office the next morning he was surprised to see his colleagues greet him effusively. In the past they would have offered no more than a polite nod when he walked by. When they met to prepare the report he needed to send his boss, he was surprised at how engaged they seemed to be. They were coming up with ideas and helping him look at things he may have missed. He remembered all the times he had asked them to stay behind for late-night meetings and how he constantly harangued them to come up with new ideas. Now, those ideas seemed to be overflowing. Mayukh had always thought of himself as being a fair boss, but wondered how letting them go home on time one day could have made such a difference.

He sent off the report to his boss well before lunch, and needed no reminder from the virus to step out for lunch with his team. Mayukh had worked with some of them for years, yet he realized that every time he met them he learnt something new about them. In turn, he started doing something he had never done before – sharing a little bit about himself. He had grown up in a culture where bosses kept their distance, but he now found himself enjoying the time he spent with his team.

When he was walking back to his cubicle, he received a text message from Sudha, reminding him to reconfirm his appointment with the doctor the next day. Mayukh groaned. This was something he had been trying hard to avoid. He knew he was no longer as young as he used to be, and a walk up a flight of stairs left him winded more often than not. He had also put on weight, and just last year he had tried on the suit he had worn at his wedding and could not even squeeze into it. In six years he had lost the physique of his youth. But was there really the need to see a doctor? Sudha kept sending him articles about the perils of middle age on one's health and telling him that he needed to be extra careful with his. But Mayukh reasoned with himself: he was just in his early thirties, and a little extra weight wasn't reason enough to spend half a day sitting in the doctor's office.

Mayukh got back to his desk to find a new box of business cards waiting for him. It was strange that his secretary had called for more because he still had a lot of them left and didn't need new ones. He wondered if someone else's cards had been left in his cubicle by mistake, and opened the box to take out one card. It had his name all right, but with an odd job title below it.

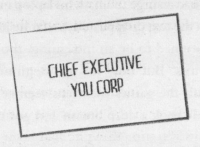

He walked over to his secretary and asked her about the weird job title. She looked at it, and then opened her email, clicking on a message from him in which he had instructed her to get new cards printed with this particular designation. Mayukh couldn't for the life of him remember having sent such a strange request and was about to ask her to throw away the cards, when something struck him. He realized that the mysterious email with these instructions must have been sent by the virus!

Damn. Mayukh cursed the virus as he walked back to his cubicle. He looked at his laptop and, as he predicted, the familiar white screen was back with another line of text.

Mayukh had an urge to smash his laptop into smithereens, but just then the text disappeared. So far he had played along with what seemed to be an intriguing, though seemingly harmless, virus. But now he was beginning to lose his patience with the games the virus seemed to be playing with him. He took a deep breath and got back to work.

The afternoon went by uneventfully but Mayukh couldn't shake off the worry that his laptop would shut down at six again, so he quickly saved all his work. He then opened his Internet browser to check the stock price. The company's stock was rising modestly, but had been quite volatile in the current economic environment. He made a mental note of when to cash in on some of his old stock options, when the graph suddenly changed before his eyes. The company's name was gone and was replaced by a puzzling title.

Mayukh could not make any sense of this, and was sure the virus was wreaking havoc on his laptop again when the white screen briefly appeared with a line of text.

How's your stock doing?

Then the graph was back, and as Mayukh moved his cursor over the part of the graph that had a sharp upward swing, a pop-up appeared with the words, 'The day you got married'. Another upswing had a pop-up announcing, 'The birth of your son'.

It took him a minute, but he began to understand what this apparent hokey was about.

The message the virus was sending him was clear. Sure he worked for a corporation, but more importantly, he ran his own corporation. His life. And if he were the Chief Executive of such an enterprise, it made sense that his stock rose at the big positive milestones of his life.

At the same time, Mayukh was worried that he might also be losing his mind for thinking that a virus was giving him advice about his life.

As unreal as it seemed, Mayukh was now so intrigued that he began to learn more about what the graph showed. The first thing he noticed was that there were clear ups and downs, but the overall trend was unmistakable.

The graph was headed downwards.

He now saw the date markers on the X-axis and clicked on the time he had last been promoted. Sure enough, there was a nice blip upwards, but this was followed by a sharp decline. This puzzled him, and he clicked on that area. He saw several pop-ups declaring: 'You missed your anniversary because you were travelling for work', 'You cancelled your vacation because of work', 'Your father wanted your help with something but you couldn't make it because of work'.

Mayukh sat back in his chair, thinking hard about what he had just seen. As he digested it all, realization began to dawn upon him. His work had clearly taken over his entire life. He had been so immersed in his career and his need to succeed at it that he had started taking the rest of his life, especially his family, for granted. He had no idea how much to read into the graph – after all, it was the virus – but the gravity of the message was suffocating him.

He noticed a tab below the graph reading, 'Key Shareholders'. He clicked on it and saw a list. At the top of that list sat Sudha, followed by Aadi, his parents, his friends, his team at the office, his boss and so on. But what was clear was that his family was, by far, the largest 'shareholder' in this corporation. So, even if he did brilliantly at work, if he compromised on what needed to be done for his largest shareholders his 'stock price' would plunge.

He evaluated the graph again and noticed that after his promotion and increased responsibilities, the graph had only plunged deeper. Mayukh sat in silence, thinking through it all and wondering what the virus wanted him to do. He was only working hard so that he could give his family the best and make sure they were happy, so why was this virus giving him such a hard time about it? Sure, he didn't have enough time for them, but one day it would get better, and then he could spend all of his time with them. And the only way to achieve that was if he worked his way up to the top now. He was, after all, just doing his damned job! But he felt a pang of shame as he scanned the various dips in the graph and all the times when he had let the shareholders of You Corp down, when it would have taken but a small gesture to delight them. Just then the omniscient virus was back with another of its one-liners.

You manage portfolios so well at work; how about managing You Corp for a change?

That really struck a chord with Mayukh. At work, he had learnt to master managing multiple projects, multiple product lines, multiple stakeholders and resources to deliver on business goals. Yet he couldn't seem to juggle any of his domestic responsibilities. What You Corp needed was just a little bit of that thinking – getting a plan to manage his portfolio of shareholders better. Mayukh suddenly got a boost of energy. He loved a challenge, and this seemed like the most worthwhile challenge life (or the virus) could have ever thrown at him – the challenge of ensuring that he never let his family down. There were two calls he needed to make immediately. The first was to his doctor, confirming his appointment, and the second to Sudha, telling her that he would be home by seven at the latest.

She was delighted at the news. Mayukh hung up and went back to his laptop. He smiled at the minor change that was staring him in the face. There was a small upward move in the graph.

Mayukh chuckled to himself at how much easier it was to work on You Corp's stock than his business at work. The smallest gesture for your biggest shareholders had an instant impact on your stock. You Corp's stock growth did not require years of R&D, mega-budget launches or celebrity endorsements. It required just a phone call, a meal together and being there when your shareholders needed you. He smiled as he turned off his laptop and headed out. His colleagues watched Mayukh leave, puzzled at their boss's rather odd behaviour. They had never seen Mayukh leave work before them. And that, too, for two consecutive days!

He drove home, barely listening to the music that blared out of the radio, his mind elsewhere. Mayukh mulled over the company called You Corp and the virus that was either driving him insane or causing him to have one epiphany after another. And perhaps there was not much difference between the two. Business school, years of late nights, hard-earned promotions, fancier job titles, bigger cubicles, bigger cars, bigger houses, fuller bank balances, and all of it perhaps amounting to not much more than an emptier life.

And a declining graph, as far as the stock price of You Corp was concerned.

When he got home, the door was already open, welcoming him back. If the company he owned was You Corp, then this was its headquarters, was it not? Why was it then that he spent infinitely more time in his cubicle than he did in the room where his son slept and played?

He found Sudha whipping up something in the kitchen and quietly hugged her from behind. She squealed at the surprise hug, and Mayukh couldn't help but burst into laughter. There was more joy in working harder for You Corp than just watching an abstract graph climb up or down.

That evening as Mayukh watched cartoons on the TV with his son, he realized that he had not had a satisfying day like this in a long time.

At night, out of habit more than anything else, he turned on his BlackBerry and saw two emails that he needed to respond to. As he hammered out his replies, he noticed Sudha out of the corner of his eye. She had a smile on her face, but her eyes said much more. They spoke of the unexpected delight of having him back home and so engaged in his family for a change, and also of the grudging acceptance that some things would not change – like his compulsive desire to check his BlackBerry at night. He turned on his laptop, not for work, but to check on

You Corp's fortunes. To his delight, Mayukh saw that the graph was now treading steadily upwards.

It had been less than a day since he had discovered that he had a job on top of what he thought of as his day job – as the Chief Executive of the corporation that was his life, and that his biggest shareholders were those whom he often left behind in pursuing his day job. The screen turned white, and Mayukh waited for the message.

You may be the CEO of You Corp but if you don't turn this off right now, there's no doubt you'll be sleeping on the couch tonight

Mayukh burst into laughter and turned his laptop off. He turned to look at Sudha who was now giving him the raised eyebrow. Whatever this virus was, it seemed to know his life inside out and seemed to be trying hard to change it. It definitely had a sense of humour as well. Mayukh was now curious about what messages the next day would bring. But for now, he went to his wife, and didn't need to look at a graph to know that You Corp's stock was doing just fine…at least for the moment.

THE NET PRESENT VALUE
OF HAPPINESS

'The revolution is not an apple that falls when it is ripe. You have to make it fall.'

CHE GUEVARA

THE NET PRESENT VALUE
OF HAPPINESS

The next morning Mayukh woke up to a barrage of emails from his boss. Fiddling with his BlackBerry, he started thinking of excuses that he could offer Sudha for not seeing the doctor. But with the morning rush to get to work on time, he decided to think of something later.

At work, Anupam, the Finance Manager, walked up to him and they began talking of the presentation they had to make to the Managing Director soon. It was about Project Pocketbook and its major stumbling block — the high initial investments, which meant that the Net Present Value of the project was always going to be low, unless they could find a way of getting the first couple of years' sales projections to be much higher than was currently the case. And that was why Mayukh and his marketing team had been working overtime — to come up with ideas on how they could conjure up sales.

Anupam groaned as he complained about how he would run things differently if he were at the top and how the present management was just too focused on short-term profits. And then, the two of them indulged in that cleansing ritual shared by cubicle dwellers the world over —

catharsis by the coffee machine. Or, to use a less fancy, but no less accurate, title – bitching about the boss.

It helped them give vent to their frustration. But, as Mayukh had learnt after so many years of working, it ultimately made little difference, since all the solutions to their problems existed in a hypothetical future where they would change the way things were run. Then it was back to the cubicle and back to the grind.

Mayukh got back to his cubicle and started trawling through the emails that he had to respond to. He was in the middle of a sentence, when the screen went white. He cursed out loud, causing his secretary to wince.

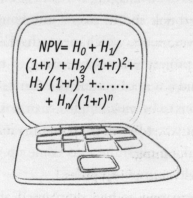

$$NPV = H_0 + H_1/(1+r) + H_2/(1+r)^2 + H_3/(1+r)^3 + \ldots\ldots + H_n/(1+r)^n$$

Mayukh rubbed his head in exasperation, as he tried to make sense of what seemed to be a mathematical puzzle. He was momentarily relieved when the bizarre equation disappeared, but before he could finish the email he had begun to write, the screen went white again and another line of text appeared.

The Pursuit of Happyness

Mayukh was about to curse again, when something struck him. It was the title of a movie he had once watched, in which H stood for Happiness. So what did that mean? It was apparent that the strange equation the virus had flashed on his screen was another twist to the mind games it so seemed to enjoy playing with him.

He thought about it for a minute, but still did not get it. Just then Anupam walked by his cubicle, mumbling something about the NPV of the project, and it hit Mayukh like a flash of lightning.

Net Present Value of Happiness!

The equation represented the Net Present Value of Happiness. But what in God's name did that mean, and why was the virus telling him about the value of happiness?

He did not get much of a chance to dwell upon the matter, because just then his boss called him over, and for the next half an hour he found himself at the receiving end of a long lecture on how the project that he was leading was hardly in a shape where they could hope for an approval from the Managing Director. Mayukh came back to his cubicle, fuming as he recalled his conversation with Anupam. If and when he got to a more senior position, he would try and help his people out, rather than just demand for more and more. When he became the boss, he would...

That's when he stopped himself. He suddenly realized what the equation for the NPV of Happiness was trying to tell him.

When he got back to his cubicle, Mayukh found the equation displayed on his laptop screen once again, and as he looked at it, he was clear on what he thought it meant.

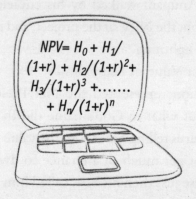

$$NPV = H_0 + H_1/(1+r) + H_2/(1+r)^2 + H_3/(1+r)^3 + \ldots\ldots + H_n/(1+r)^n$$

It basically showed H_n as the happiness created in year n, with 0 being the current year and n being the number of years you live. In the equation, as with any NPV calculation, r was the rate at which future value is discounted, simply because there is a time premium associated with any value – something enjoyed now is better than something enjoyed later. That was the whole concept behind Net Present Value – something he had learnt a long time ago at business school, and then at work, but had never thought about applying to something as basic as happiness.

The way the equation worked was that the first year has the highest weight, as its value is not discounted. The further into the future you go, the lesser the contribution of any one year, given that each succeeding year is discounted at a compounded rate. It was based on the simple theory that present gains were always more valued than hypothetical future gains. So money earned today would mean more than the same amount promised a year later.

The meaning of the NPV of Happiness was clear. Planning or thinking of all the big things you may do in the future does not bring you as much happiness as, perhaps, a smaller gesture today. Mayukh looked back at the last couple of days and realized just how true that was. He had spent years working late, with few vacations, and kept assuring his wife (and himself) that they would go on a big holiday the next year. He realized that for him and his wife, and indeed the stock valuation of You Corp, such nebulous future plans meant less than just being there on time to have dinner with his family.

And then he thought about what he had put off doing that morning. He had promised his wife that he would go to the doctor but then had quietly resolved to put it off. He had not told her that he had not yet taken leave or set aside time to attend Aadi's school function the following day. Sure, he might well take his family for a vacation to Europe in six months' time, but letting them down on such seemingly small occasions would perhaps hurt them more than any promise of future joy could compensate for.

On the other hand, now that he knew what he wasn't doing, he had the power of changing that.

Getting down to business immediately, Mayukh told his surprised secretary that he was going out of the office for a couple of hours, and called his doctor. The visit was not something that necessarily cheered him up, but he realized that it was perhaps something that he needed to hear. He was overweight, his cholesterol was high, his blood pressure was on the higher side and, if he didn't want to have heart problems or diabetes later on in life, he needed to act now.

Mayukh knew all of this in theory. It was acting on it that was tough. He had kept promising himself that he'd get some exercise when the pressure at work was not so high, but that time never seemed to come.

It seemed that the equation could equally represent the NPV of Health.

Having spent the two hours away from his cubicle meant that he worked on overdrive for the rest of the afternoon. He never noticed that, even without the laptop screen turning blank in the evening, he subconsciously paced himself so that he was pretty much done for the day by six. He was about to power off his laptop when his boss walked by, rattling off some data that he needed first thing in the morning. Mayukh felt a stab of panic. The NPV of Happiness was well and good, and he had already resolved to be at his son's event in the morning. He wanted to have dinner with his family as well, but how could he possibly do any of that if he had to meet his boss's last-minute request?

As he sat mulling, there was a tap on his shoulder. It was one of his colleagues. The young man asked him if he needed any help, and Mayukh told him honestly what was on his mind. Just a few days ago it would have been inconceivable, but spending more time with his team had made him open up to them much more. To his surprise, the young man smiled and said that he'd get the data and send it to Mayukh's boss. Mayukh thanked him and was about to pack up for the day with a smile on his face, when his laptop screen flashed him one last message.

You Corp is not a one-man shop. We are all partners in each other's corporations.

After a lovely family dinner, Mayukh broke the news to his wife.

'Sudha, about Aadi's school function tomorrow...'

He had not even completed the sentence when he saw her downcast expression. No doubt she thought he would let them down again, saying that he had a meeting to attend to at work, so he hastened to add – 'I'll be there with you.'

Sudha beamed and Aadi looked up at Mayukh with his wide, innocent eyes.

'Daddy, won't you be going to the office?'

When Mayukh shook his head, Aadi laughed in delight, and that was more than enough to tell Mayukh just how much joy he had brought into You Corp.

They spent the next morning watching a bunch of toddlers perform their own version of the *Wizard of Oz* on stage, with Aadi playing the role of the Cowardly Lion. When Mayukh dropped his family home, with Aadi staying true to his part and constantly roaring, and drove to the office, he realized that he could barely remember the last time he had felt this good about his life.

This virus called the Cubicle Manifesto seemed to have changed his life remarkably in a short period of time. Mayukh was happier, his people at work were happier and, most importantly, his family was happier. There was one problem though. Granted, he had realized what really mattered when it came to creating value for You Corp. Granted, he now knew that it was better to act now, instead of waiting for some elusive future happiness and, granted, he now knew that his work was hardly the only thing that he could count on to bring him satisfaction.

The big problem was one of time.

It wasn't as if his responsibilities at work had shrunk in any way. If anything, with the presentation to the Managing Director looming over the horizon, and with all the hurdles that afflicted the project he was working on, work over the next few days was going to be tough. So even if he did manage to leave the office at a decent hour, or rather, be forced to by the virus, how was he ever going to carve out time for other things?

When he had told his wife about what the doctor had said, her joy at his actually having gone to see him rapidly gave way to mounting concern. One thing Mayukh loved about her was that she rarely nagged, but what she left unsaid was clear. They both knew that Mayukh would need to make time to exercise. The problem here again was that he had no idea how he would ever make time for it. With the traffic, the pressure at work and the fact that he needed to be with his family to make You Corp a success, how was he expected to make any time for himself?

That feeling was only reinforced when he came to the office the next day and saw a long list of things that he had to accomplish in the day. He girded himself and got down to work, his mind on little else other than ticking off the dozen items on his to-do list before the virus decided it was time for him to head home.

For once, the virus seemed to understand the pressure that he was under, and sent no reminder for him to step out for lunch. Out of curiosity, Mayukh clicked on the shortcut icon for the You Corp stock and saw that it was still rising. So the message was not that he didn't need to work and just spend time with his family. It was all about balance – he could skip lunch, if he needed to, to get urgent work done with no negative impact on You Corp, because he had used the time to be with his family when they needed him.

Just before he left for home, Anupam stopped by at his desk.

'Mayukh, I was wondering if you were still working on Project Pocketbook?'

Mayukh was surprised by the sudden question, and said he was. To which Anupam responded with an even stranger question.

'Are you aware of the rumours that are circulating about you?'

Now Mayukh was truly intrigued.

'What rumours, Anupam?'

Anupam leant conspiratorially over the cubicle wall, his ample paunch threatening to spill out of his shirt.

'They say you are looking out for something better. Perhaps you already have a job offer…'

Mayukh was too shocked to say anything, so he motioned to Anupum to sit down. Anupam may have been good at his work, but one thing that Mayukh never liked about him was his desire to get ahead – even if it meant stepping over others. Mayukh now began to suspect where those rumours may have been originating from.

'You see, Mayukh, everyone's talking. People know the shape Project Pocketbook is in, and my neck is on the line too, but I can only do so much. It's the marketing plan that isn't working. Add to that the fact that you're taking so many breaks and going home early. It's only natural that people will talk.'

Mayukh didn't quite know how to explain what he was going through, and settled for a convenient lie that he was working from home. As he began to leave and closed the office door behind him, he saw Anupam still hunched over a spreadsheet at his cubicle. He realized that understanding the best possible application of the concept of NPV did not require you to be a Finance Manager.

MAKING AN APPOINTMENT WITH YOURSELF

'We must use time wisely and forever realize that the time is always ripe to do right.'

NELSON MANDELA

Next day, Mayukh managed to finish all his work and leave for home just after six. He was relieved that the virus was cutting him some slack and had not turned off his laptop at six. When he reached home, he noticed something that he had never paid attention to before. Perhaps it was just the fact that the appointment with the doctor had made him more aware, but he realized that he was breathing heavily after climbing just one flight of stairs. Mayukh had never been an athlete, but before joining work he had been in pretty decent shape. Years of long hours at work, eating junk food and no exercise at all had clearly taken its toll.

After dinner that evening, he reached into the freezer for some ice cream, but stopped. Sudha perhaps sensed his dilemma and handed him a scoop with a smile. As they were watching TV, Mayukh began to think of what the doctor had told him. If he was so worried about his family's future, what purpose would it serve if he was not healthy enough to fully enjoy it with them? What irritated

Mayukh was that he knew how to solve the problem but he wasn't doing anything to rectify it. It was just a matter of how he could find the time for himself to get some exercise.

Next morning when he reached the office, the first thing that he did was to boot up his laptop and scan his calendar. As usual, it was fairly packed. Even as he sighed, his secretary came over to tell him about two more meetings that had been requested by some agencies. Mayukh quickly studied his calendar for the next few days and told her where to slot them in.

He wondered, 'How would I ever survive at work without my calendar?'

For the rest of the day, the virus left him alone to get his work done, but by evening he was faced with a familiar dilemma. His calendar was so packed with meetings to attend, calls to make and things to do that the day seemed to whizz by faster than he could imagine. He felt like he had no control over it. That again reminded him just how difficult it was to find any time for himself – either to get that much-needed exercise or to even finish off the odd errands like paying bills online or attending to financial matters or following up on work at home. He had been chasing after workmen to get a few repairs done at his home, but with the hectic schedule at the office it meant that everything had to wait till after he left work – with the result that he had to get his personal errands done on the way home in his car, or at night or on weekends. Either way, he felt like he never got any breathing space. He was human after all!

As if reading his mind, his screen turned white.

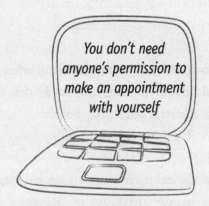

You don't need anyone's permission to make an appointment with yourself

The virus, Mayukh thought, was not some fortune-telling genie. After all, the message was silly as hell. Of course he did not need anyone else's permission. It was obvious as breathing air, so why this simple message after all the incisive others?

Mayukh needed to begin working, but he knew it was useless trying to get rid of the taunting voice of the message. In a minute, another line popped up on the screen.

Don't be a slave to your own calendar

Mayukh still couldn't get his head around what the virus was trying to tell him or getting him to do this time, and was happy when the messages disappeared.

At night, as was his habit, he turned on his BlackBerry to check for any urgent messages or meetings that he'd have to attend early next morning, and also to study his calendar so that he could be mentally prepared for the day ahead. As his screen flickered to life and he clicked on the calendar icon, he saw a couple of puzzling things.

From seven to seven-thirty in the morning, his calendar was blocked with a meeting. He groaned as he wondered why his boss had called for such an early-morning meeting, but when he saw the details he was even more confused. The calendar entry read:

And there were no other attendees.

As he looked at the rest of his day, he saw another similar appointment – this time, only fifteen minutes long and scheduled just after lunch. A meeting he had with a colleague had been pushed back fifteen minutes to fit this in.

Mayukh scrolled down and saw that the two appointments appeared in his calendar not just for the following day but on every other weekday that followed. There was nobody else who had access to his calendar other than his secretary and he could not fathom why she would possibly put such entries in his calendar. Then Mayukh realized that it could only be one thing.

The virus.

So it had now decided to take over his BlackBerry too. Mayukh wondered for a second if it was healthy to be paying heed to this virus, or if he was losing his sanity. Surely people would think he had gone mad if he told anyone that a virus was giving him life advice? Or what if there was something else at play, something much bigger than a virus? It was not as if the virus was bringing up things that Mayukh had never considered. Of course, he knew the stress that his work hours caused to his personal life and he knew how his health had been deteriorating. What the virus was doing was holding a mirror up to Mayukh, forcing him to see his choices for what they were and what they were leading to. It was not very different from a person neglecting a weight problem till a close friend tells them that they have put on weight. Was the virus just bringing to life those uncomfortable truths for Mayukh?

Too tired for answers, Mayukh slipped into a fitful sleep.

At a quarter to seven in the morning, Mayukh was rudely awoken by the alarm on his BlackBerry. He could have sworn he had turned it off before he went to sleep, and as he reached over he saw that the phone was indeed off. As he watched, the screen flickered to life with a morning message.

Good morning, Champ. Time for you to meet yourself. Don't be late!

Mayukh cursed the virus for having woken him up so early and wondered what it possibly wanted him to do at this hour. But the minute he asked himself the question, the answer presented itself. Of course...

He had been agonizing over how he could possibly find time in his packed calendar to exercise, and here it was. After so many years of working, Mayukh had been conditioned to run his life through his calendar and to-do lists. If something was on them, he would make sure he got it done. But if something was not on it, there was little or no chance that he would get around to doing it.

That's what the virus was trying to tell him. Rather than fight his calendar and be a victim who merely showed up for appointments others foisted on him, he had to start using his calendar to take charge of his own time. If he needed to exercise, rather than make vague promises, he needed to approach it no differently than how he managed to deal with the other demands on his time – put it on his calendar.

As he got dressed and went down to the gym in the apartment complex, Mayukh realized just how much the virus had him figured out. The mere fact that the 'appointment with himself' was on his calendar, and with an accompanying alarm, meant that he was approaching it more seriously than he would ever have if the desire to exercise had remained a nebulous promise in his mind.

As he ran on the treadmill, he realized once again just how out of shape he was. Within ten minutes of jogging, he was huffing and puffing, and his lungs felt like they would burst. He thought of just turning off the treadmill and ending the torture, but he persevered, driven by the knowledge that so far whatever the virus had put him through had only had a positive outcome.

An hour later, as Mayukh walked back home, sweating and with aching legs, there was no ignoring the rush of adrenalin which made him feel energetic, clear in the head and keyed up. He left for work that morning thanking the virus for the first time.

Time flew by and when Mayukh came back to his cubicle after lunch with a few colleagues, he saw that his laptop just would not turn on. His BlackBerry, too, seemed to be dead. He asked his secretary what appointments he had and she told him that he had indicated in his calendar that he was not to be disturbed at all for fifteen minutes. Then he remembered that the virus had gone ahead and put in another appointment with himself just after lunch. This made no sense to Mayukh. The morning appointment in his calendar had clearly served a purpose. It was designed to ensure that he got disciplined about exercising, but what earthly purpose could this fifteen-minute appointment serve?

When he walked back to his cubicle, he saw that the virus was back.

Just 15 minutes for yourself each day adds up. Do the maths, Genius.

With nothing else to do, Mayukh did precisely what the virus was asking him to do. If he had fifteen minutes set aside every day that would equal to more than ninety hours every year! With the amount of time he had been working, that added up to more than a month of extra time over his career so far. But time to do what?

Mayukh grinned. He had his answer. It was all the odd errands that he struggled to remember or cope with. All the individually small, yet collectively important cogs of running the machine called his home and life that he somehow never found time for or ended up doing late at night or on weekends. If he just took out fifteen minutes every day, he could wrap all of them up without compromising in any way what he had to deliver at work.

As Mayukh made the first phone call to a workman who needed to come over and fix their kitchen door, he decided to make a note of what he would achieve every day in those fifteen minutes that the virus had just gifted him. His laptop came back to life, and within minutes his calendar was populated. The fifteen minutes he had every day was soon filled with notes and reminders – people to call, things to do, bills to pay. There was no way he could forget now, and also there was no longer any excuse for pretending that he did not have time for doing any of those things.

The virus had just taught him a valuable lesson; one that Mayukh mentally kicked himself for never having figured out in all these years of working. He had learnt to be capable of running multimillion-dollar budgets and projects by structuring them and using his calendar to ensure that he did not slip on deadlines or fail to meet commitments. All it took was adopting a little bit of discipline and using that very same calendar to be able to make time for himself and to keep his commitments to himself.

So far he had thought of work and his work calendar as somehow totally divorced from the rest of his life. But if he just used that same tool to try and fit in some of the things he needed to do for himself, it seemed to unlock possibilities where he had previously seen none.

He was about to leave for home when his boss stopped by. Mayukh got a long monologue, but the upshot was that he wanted him to think 'out of the box'. That was the only way he thought Project Pocketbook could work. Anupam, who had clearly overheard the conversation, came by soon after. He had a smug, I-told-you-so expression on his face that made Mayukh want to punch his lights out, but he settled for listening quietly to another lecture from him. Mayukh had almost tuned out, but when he paid attention he was glad he did, for he heard him close his lecture with a zinger.

'You see, Mayukh, this project looks like it will not fly, and I have sent through a recommendation to the MD that the financial viability is suspect unless we get a marketing breakthrough.'

Mayukh looked at Anupam, now clearly seeing the political games he was up to. In one email, Anupam had managed to cover his ass and put all possible blame for the failure of the project on Mayukh's shoulders.

'Mayukh, I was talking to some people in your team and, you know, I thought you guys could look at the data in a different way. I've passed on some tips to them.'

Mayukh groaned inwardly. All he needed was for Anupam to now tell him how to do his job.

Mayukh drove home, feeling much of his earlier optimism dissipate. With all the pressure of work, a packed calendar, deadlines to meet and now with all the virus had taught him about taking care of You Corp's shareholders and creating time for himself, where did one get time for 'out of the box' ideas? He and his people had given the project their very best shot, and had used all the available data and hours of brainstorming to get their best ideas on the table. Unfortunately, none of it seemed to be good enough. Mayukh sighed. Life had a funny way of kicking you in the shins and having a good laugh about it sometimes.

MAXIM FIVE

WHEN YOU DO NOTHING AT ALL

'Human salvation lies in the hands of the creatively maladjusted.'

MARTIN LUTHER KING, JR.

Mayukh entered the office the next morning with mixed emotions.

Part of him was glad that it was a Friday. With the week he had just been through, and with the havoc the virus had wreaked in his life, all he wanted to do was to forget it all for two days, before he had to confront the pressure again next Monday. However, the other part of him dreaded coming to the office for this one day. The harsh feedback his boss had given him last evening was still fresh in his mind, and he really had no idea of how he was going to salvage the project before their big meeting.

So he spent the morning doing what he had been trained to do. What two years of business school and years of cubicle dwelling had ingrained in him – that the best way to solve a problem was to immerse oneself in data and hope that charts and graphs could somehow conjure up the inspiration that one sought.

He called his team over for a meeting just before lunch, and saw that they were even more stressed out than he was. They had run all the numbers, spent countless hours rechecking assumptions, run statistical models, but nothing seemed to offer a way out. As his dispirited team walked back to their cubicles, Mayukh felt self-doubt gnawing him. Perhaps he had been foolhardy to champion this project in the first place. Perhaps the project really was doomed. Those were things he could only conjecture about. What was certain was that when the project crashed and burned, it would likely take his career with it.

Mayukh ate lunch in silence at his cubicle, glad that the virus was leaving him in peace. With the kind of mood he was in, Mayukh did not doubt that he could really pick up his laptop and throw it out the window if the virus reappeared. He had been through a lot of positive things in the week gone by – making the time to know his team, spending more time with his family, learning to carve out time for himself – but, ultimately, if his career was going to be doomed, did any of that matter? Maybe Anupam was right after all. Maybe he should just be spending more time in the office and try to get some new ideas from his team. He felt a headache coming, and wished that he could just go home and forget about all his worries.

He spent a few more minutes looking at all the research reports and all the data his team had churned out. His employer manufactured and marketed a wide range of consumer electronics, and the project he had been working on was a new line of low-cost ultraportable laptops. When the project had been conceived by their global headquarters a couple of years ago, it had seemed like a brilliant idea and Mayukh had volunteered to lead it.

However, the recent explosion of tablet computers had made it seem less and less likely that the idea would ever reach the potential that he had imagined for it. Perhaps he should just have cut his losses and recommended to his management that the idea should be abandoned. But the R&D dollars already spent, and his own credibility being on the line, had made him flinch at doing so. Their product was affordable and very light and portable, but nobody had yet come up with an idea of how it could survive in the face of the seemingly endless onslaught of tablet computers. His own company was no exception, and was readying a line of tablet computers to be launched. Mayukh was at his wits' end. There was no more research he could think of commissioning, no more ways of slicing and dicing the data that he could come up with. In short, he was out of ideas, and fast running out of time.

He massaged his temples with his fingers, trying to ease away the headache and think of how he could go up to his boss and confess that he had messed up monumentally and still keep his job. Oh, God, I need an answer, thought Mayukh.

That was when his screen turned white.

Sometimes it's best to do nothing at all

Mayukh glared at the screen in fury, ready to smash his laptop to pieces. 'Not now,' he muttered under his breath and scrambled to turn it off, but no key he pressed seemed to have an effect.

When his screen finally came back to normal, Mayukh looked up, puzzled to see his team gathered around his cubicle. He asked them what they wanted, and they told him that they had come for the meeting he had called for. He was about to ask them to grab a nearby meeting room when his secretary came over and told him that she had arranged for a cab to take them for the meeting.

Mayukh had no idea what she was talking about, and then saw that in his calendar the meeting had been set up at a nearby shopping mall. The meeting agenda, if one could call it that, was first to meet at a coffee shop and then to walk around the mall. Mayukh could see that his colleagues were exchanging glances, wary at what he was up to, and wondered what the virus was making him do. But having seen it produce some good results so far, Mayukh decided to play along.

At the coffee shop, Mayukh and his team sat around sipping their coffee without any sort of enlightenment. He could see that his team members, who were making small talk among themselves, were confused about what they were expected to do. The calendar entry had been explicit in its instructions – no laptops, no slides, no paper. They were to just drink some coffee and watch. So Mayukh did precisely that.

He watched the people who were there at the coffee shop. A motley crew of students, women, businessmen and shoppers. The students, who seemed to have come from a neighbouring college, were buried in their laptops, busy working on their assignments. Mayukh liked the way the students were so absorbed in their work. It reminded him of the days when he was in business school, burning the midnight oil in some café with his friends. It felt exactly the same, with one exception. 'Boy, these kids sure have a lot of gadgets these days,' thought Mayukh. Most of the students had smartphones, one or two of them had tablet computers, but every one of them had a laptop. He watched the boy who had both a tablet and a laptop and wondered what the need was to have both. There was only one way to find out.

Mayukh got up and strode over to the group and introduced himself. He asked them why they had so many devices. A boy shrugged at his question and replied, 'Well, tablets are cool to surf the Net or download music, 'cause they are handy and slim. It makes sense carrying it around. But when I need to get work done, I need a laptop 'cause of the keyboard...essentially a lot of spreadsheets and other software we use are much easier to use on a laptop.'

It was that simple. Mayukh thanked them and jogged back to his table. 'I've got it, guys.'

They sat at the coffee shop, each of them browsing for information on their phones. One of his teammates spoke up triumphantly.

'I have a list of colleges here that give laptops to their students. We could target them with bulk sales, couldn't we?'

'Brilliant idea! What else can we do, guys?'

'Mayukh, we could pre-bundle it with software students need. A lot of them are pretty expensive on their own, but we could get bulk discounts from the software firms and bundle those as a big added value.'

As they finished their coffee and went to get a cab back to the office, they passed a bank and one of them stopped.

'You know what else we missed? We can target students, but they won't have huge amounts of cash. We could tie up with a bank to provide interest–free instalments.'

As they continued, Mayukh was keeping a running tally of all the ideas that he was burning to write down as soon as he got back to the office.

Back in his cubicle, Mayukh jotted down everything they had talked about, and when he met his team he could see a palpable change in their mood. They still didn't know if their idea would salvage the project, but for the first time in months they could see a flicker of hope.

And all it had required was for him to get away from his cubicle, to get away from what was usually considered 'work', and sit and watch people while drinking coffee. To do, as the virus had said, nothing at all.

Not bad, thought Mayukh. Not bad at all.

The next three hours went by in a blur as they put all their ideas together and had a skeleton of the presentation ready. They were to meet the Managing Director on the coming Wednesday and Mayukh told them that they would meet again on Monday to fine-tune their proposal, and also to take his boss through the ideas that they had.

Anupam stopped by Mayukh's cubicle, carrying a sheaf of printouts of the financials of Project Pocketbook.

'Mayukh, I hear you and your team are taking a lot of coffee breaks. They seemed pretty happy with the idea, but I don't know if they've seen how terrible the financials look.'

Mayukh sat him down and ran him through the ideas they had come up with. Anupam's jaw literally dropped. Pleased with the effect, Mayukh smiled and capped it all by saying that a cup of coffee could do wonders for the quality of ideas.

As a puzzled Anupam left, Mayukh saw that the virus had a new message for him.

To think out of the box, take yourself out of your box

He smiled and before packing up for the day, he set up a time slot in his calendar for coffee with his team every Friday evening in the nearby café. If just one day of getting out of the usual confines of the office and the usual way of approaching things could have given them so many new ideas, what more could they achieve if they did so on a more regular basis?

As he drove home, Mayukh again smiled to himself. He realized that being in the box, in the usual setting of office cubicles and meeting rooms, often meant that he subconsciously reverted to using the crutches of corporate life – PowerPoint slides, numbers, charts – to try and make up for ideas. They were just tools to express and refine ideas, but they could not provide the inspiration that one could get when one just stepped out of the box and took the time to observe people and what was happening around oneself.

When people talked of getting 'out of the box' ideas, the one thing they often failed to realize was that to truly think out of the box, a good starting point would perhaps be to take *oneself* out of the box in the first place.

Amid all these thoughts, Mayukh was curious why the virus had picked him and how it operated. Why him? Far from being the malicious virus he had initially suspected it to be, it had showed him so many new ways of approaching his work and his life that in just a week his life was barely recognizable from what it had once been.

He turned on the radio in the car and sang along as he drove home. Life sure was strange.

TURNING OFF THE BLINKING RED LIGHT OF SERVITUDE

'There is no such thing as part freedom.'

NELSON MANDELA

The weekend began on a pleasant note, with a trip to the nearby park where Mayukh and his family played a game of Frisbee, fed the ducks on the lake and topped it all with a scrumptious picnic. As they were walking, Mayukh just stopped and looked around with a smile on his face.

'Mayukh, what are you looking at?'

He didn't respond, and instead continued smiling and joined Sudha. As they continued walking, he couldn't help basking in the joy of just being outside with his family, feeling the wind in his hair, breathing the fresh air and watching Aadi run around on the grass.

Later, they headed to the movies to catch the new animated film which had just hit the theatres. In short, it was an afternoon that his son couldn't stop talking about.

As Mayukh sat in the darkened theatre, he pulled out his BlackBerry…just to check. And, sure enough, he was greeted with the familiar blinking light. It was one of his team, fleshing out more ideas and asking for directions on whether he should check out an additional idea. Mayukh began responding to the email when his son nudged him, asking him which car was going to win the race. Mayukh smiled at him and told him he'd be right with him, and proceeded to finish his email. When he pressed 'Send' and looked at his son, he saw that Sudha was telling him something about the movie.

Mayukh bought some popcorn and they continued watching the movie, when he saw the red light blinking again. With years of conditioning, it did not even require a conscious thought for him to pick up his BlackBerry and respond to yet another email. Sudha leaned over and whispered to him to stop working. When they had got married, she would sometimes nag him about being married to his BlackBerry, but she had given up over the years. However, today she seemed annoyed.

Mayukh had never thought much of it. Everyone did it nowadays, right? Being connected was what it was all about, wasn't it? Being able to react to a change in plans and the market was what made a manager successful, didn't it? So, for some time now, he'd had a daily ritual of checking emails every night.

But he was taken by surprise. He never worked on weekends, or at least always tried not to, and rarely, if ever, took paperwork home. Just as he began to protest that he was simply checking a few emails, the screen of the BlackBerry went white and a message appeared.

The blinking red light on your BlackBerry is the invisible leash that ties you to your cubicle

Then, to Mayukh's immense irritation, the phone died. He bit his lip so that he wouldn't curse in front of his son. Now there was nothing left to do but watch the movie.

As it turned out, it was a smashing movie! Mayukh cursed his stupidity for missing the first half.

Sunday was pleasant enough, but Mayukh's BlackBerry still refused to turn on. He wondered if his boss had replied to his email, or wanted anything for the Monday presentation. Or if his team had sent over any more ideas that they could work on. He felt cut off and disconnected, and that made him feel like he had lost control. The virus surely had this one totally wrong. Far from being a leash, his BlackBerry was more like his remote control – so that he could stay on top of his work, no matter where he was. By evening, he was checking on his BlackBerry every few minutes, and his wife said – only half jokingly – that he was behaving like a drug addict going through withdrawal symptoms.

Finally, close to bedtime, the red light began blinking again, and he picked up his BlackBerry like an excited five-year-old picking up his Christmas present.

He spent the next thirty minutes tapping out email after email. Before he turned it off, it flashed the familiar stock graph for You Corp, and Mayukh saw that his stock had declined. Turning it off, he took a deep breath and tried to control his irritation. The virus had shown him some interesting ideas and insights, but he did not need some strange virus to babysit him.

As he got into bed, he could see Sudha peering at him over the book that she was reading. Already irritated, he was about to snap at her when she asked if he was done with work, but checked himself. He didn't want to take out his anger at the virus on Sudha. Instead, he apologized for taking so much time, and went to the freezer to fetch her some ice cream. He did not need to check the stock chart to know that You Corp's value would have just risen…just a little bit.

Monday morning and Mayukh's cubicle was a beehive of activity. Feeling energetic and not overwhelmed by all the work that lay ahead of him and his team, he was glad that he had got his usual dose of early-morning exercise. His colleagues were working with a kind of energy that he had never seen before, and each of them had several ideas and leads worked out in a fair bit of detail. The meeting with his boss was just after lunch, so Mayukh decided that they would work till eleven to tie all the loose ends and then the remaining time could be used to put together the presentation.

At eleven, he and his team gathered in a meeting room. Mayukh hooked up his laptop to project the presentation flow he had prepared, so that they could simply copy and paste in the material. Seeing his colleagues look at him expectantly, and overhearing one of his teammates brag about their 'cool' project and boss to another colleague a few minutes earlier, had made Mayukh's heart swell with pride. Just a week earlier, his team had the look of a defeated army, ready to surrender. He thanked everybody for all their efforts and then pushed the button to project what was on his laptop screen.

In a high-quality video, they all saw a group of Spartans decapitate Persian elite warriors.

Mayukh's team looked on in stupefied silence, wondering if this was some new brainstorming technique he was trying out. As the movie *300* continued to play, Mayukh desperately pushed and prodded all the buttons on his laptop to stop it. It had been one of his favourite movies, and he had downloaded it onto his laptop long ago. But he had no idea how it could have suddenly started playing and then refused to stop. It could only be the work of the virus. Mayukh panicked. Was it turning evil now? After all, it was actually a virus!

He made a joke about technical glitches and asked his team to come back in five minutes as he took the battery out of his laptop to turn it off. When he turned it on again, he was seething with rage. This was going too far. With the limited time they had to prepare the presentation, this was the worst possible moment for the virus to be playing such a joke on him. When his screen flickered back to life, there was the familiar message:

If you can't watch a movie in the office, why can you email your office from home?

Mayukh sat back as he digested those words.

There were so many aspects of his personal life that he would never dream of bringing into his office, simply because he, like all other employees, had been conditioned to believe that some things were inappropriate. So he could not watch movies, read novels or play music he liked out loud. However, at home, where he didn't have his boss overseeing him, he did not operate in a similar way. He never thought twice before using his BlackBerry when he should have been focusing on his family. No wonder the stock price of You Corp had plummeted, despite him being with his family at the movie – because he was not giving them what they deserved.

After his meeting with his boss, Mayukh left feeling very good about himself and his team. His boss had been pleasantly surprised to see how the project seemed to be turning around, and complimented Mayukh and his team lavishly. Anupam looked a bit sheepish when the meeting ended, and, while it would have been quite a stretch for him to acknowledge that he had been wrong, he did the next best thing. He told Mayukh that whatever he was doing seemed to be working for the project and the team. However, not quite willing to admit that he had been totally wrong, he did add in passing that he only hoped that the Managing Director bought all the newfangled ways of doing things that Mayukh was trying to employ. Mayukh left for home feeling on top of the world.

With his BlackBerry switched off.

77

MAXIM SEVEN

REACH OUT AND TOUCH SOMEONE

'When the prison windows are opened, the real dragon will come out.'

HO CHI MINH

When Mayukh entered the office the next morning, he saw anticipation writ large on the faces of his team members. One of them asked him if he had seen all the ideas that they had been emailing to him. She seemed stunned by Mayukh's reply.

'No, actually I didn't turn on my BlackBerry last night, but as soon as I boot up my laptop, I'll go through all your ideas.'

He could tell by their puzzled faces just how surprised they were. One of them confessed that she was quite surprised not to see any emails from him at night, and had begun to wonder if Mayukh was not well. The reason why they sent him emails after office hours, she added, was because they assumed that this was the way he wanted to work, and so they were only trying to keep up with their boss. Mayukh realized just how wrong he had been. He had assumed that somehow his habits existed in a vacuum, but that was not the case. As a manager, what he did set the norms for his team, and affected them as well.

As he got down to work, Mayukh saw a chain of emails, sparked off by Anupam's report to the MD. Angry at people assuming that he was going to fail even before he got a fair chance, he was about to reply to his boss, saying that he had things under control, when his screen turned white, with a single message on it.

Ditching his earlier plan, he had settled down at his desk once again when his secretary told him, with a barely concealed smile, that all his team members were talking about the changes in him. Trying to sound casual about it, Mayukh simply said that he was following some ideas that he had read in a book.

'Everyone should probably read that book,' she said.

The morning went by in a blur of preparing slides and the final material for the meeting with the Managing Director the next day. But with the morning's interaction still fresh in his mind, Mayukh squeezed in some time to send out an email to his team, saying that while he wanted them to be fully engaged when at work, what they did after office hours was their personal choice. If any of them wanted to send emails, they could, but he would personally not check any emails after office hours. However, if there was a genuine business emergency or crisis, his team was free to call on his personal mobile phone. Just then there was another incoming message.

Reach out and touch someone

Mayukh didn't get much time to ponder the message and by the time he got back to his cubicle after all the presentation preparations, he was quite tired. He got himself a cup of coffee and then sat down to see that his laptop was displaying his calendar. A new entry showed that for the next fifteen minutes he was not supposed to have any meetings, but to 'connect'.

There were two tabs open – one for Facebook and one for LinkedIn. Mayukh really did not have the time to indulge in casual chats, so he tried to close the browser, but could not. By now he knew how persistent the virus could be, so he figured that for the next fifteen minutes he'd have little option but to do as the virus was suggesting.

He noticed that one of his old college friends had sent him an invitation to connect on Facebook. He accepted it. They chatted for the next five minutes, and the old memories flooded back.

The two of them had entertained dreams of being writers when they were in college, and then, of course, Mayukh had left those childish dreams behind and joined business school, then the corporate world, and never looked back. He was fascinated to learn that his friend had actually published a book, in addition to working for a bank.

Mayukh wondered, what had happened to his dreams?

With the fifteen minutes up, the browser closed on its own, and the virus had perhaps the most important message for Mayukh.

Nurture your connections. They remind you of who you were before you entered your cubicle.

Mayukh thought about it, and realized that in just fifteen minutes he had reconnected with one of his closest friends, who, at one point, had meant a lot to him. That in itself was valuable enough, but also what the virus had said made a lot of sense.

He guessed what the virus had in mind, and as he checked his calendar he saw that every day his calendar had an entry to 'connect' for fifteen minutes. Between the fifteen minutes after lunch and now fifteen minutes of 'connecting' – in addition to the Fridays when he was supposed to get out of the office with his team to think about tough problems in a fresh setting – Mayukh wondered how the virus expected him to get any work done.

Mayukh left the office and was about to get into his car when he felt his phone vibrate. It was a new email sent through LinkedIn. He saw that it was from an old college friend, who was a mutual friend of the guy he had just connected with earlier in the day. This friend had gone into academia and was a professor at one of the leading universities. She had just heard from their mutual friend that he had reconnected with Mayukh and learnt where he worked. She was, in addition to being a professor, also leading a few social outreach projects to help underprivileged kids. One of her ideas was to start a campaign to get affordable laptops to these kids so that they could enrich their learning and get more connected. She had been looking for corporations who might be interested in such a campaign, and when she learnt where Mayukh worked, she was wondering if he may be able to help.

Mayukh stood in the car park, his mind racing at the possibilities. With his friend being a senior professor at a leading university, their whole idea of targeting students with their new laptop could get a kickstart. He called her and they chatted for a few minutes. She was thrilled to hear that Mayukh was very keen to work together on the campaign and to help out. As it turned out, she was not just a professor at a university, but she was also on the boards of several other colleges. She said that she would send Mayukh their contact details so he could follow up with them as well.

Mayukh whipped out his BlackBerry and when it turned on he realized that the virus was okay with him sending this message. So he quickly sent some follow-up messages, one to his friend confirming that his firm would love to explore how they could partner in the campaign, and another one to his team members, telling them of this exciting new development. He added that they would meet first thing the next morning to build this possibility into the plans that they would present to the Managing Director.

Before he turned off his BlackBerry, he saw a new message from the virus.

When you connect, new possibilities will present themselves

That night he had a great dinner with his family. Later, he read a bedtime story to his son and then sat to watch TV with Sudha, who, unable to believe that her husband was not fidgeting with his BlackBerry every now and then, kept looking his way with a slightly puzzled expression.

When they went to bed, Mayukh lay awake for some time, thinking about all he had learnt. He felt healthier and happier, his family seemed to enjoy having him around more and the icing on the cake was that he was actually doing so much better at work! At the same time, he couldn't help wondering what the Cubicle Manifesto virus really was, and how it had come into his life. There was no question that it had, in a very short time, changed his life dramatically, but he still could not understand what it was and why he had never heard of it before.

As he drifted off to sleep, he thought about the dream he had once held on to with the strongest of convictions. The dream of becoming a writer. But his eyes were too heavy, and he gave in to the clutches of sleep.

MAXIM EIGHT

DON'T YOU LOVE THE SMELL OF REVOLUTION IN THE MORNING?

'We have not made the Revolution, the Revolution has made us.'

GEORG BÜCHNER

Mayukh ran an extra ten minutes on the treadmill that morning, both because he was feeling keyed up about the big presentation he had to make to the Managing Director that afternoon, and also because he found that just a week of regular exercise had done wonders for his stamina and wellbeing.

If this meeting had happened just a couple of weeks ago, Mayukh knew that he would have been a nervous wreck, perhaps staying in the office till ten or eleven, going over last-minute details, and making his team stay on till late as well. However, while he was psyched about the meeting, there was none of the usual anxiety or nervousness.

By eleven, Mayukh and his team were ready to go. He decided to use his fifteen minutes of 'connecting' then instead of after lunch. The first thing he did was to call his parents, who were surprised and delighted to hear from him after several days. After the usual pleasantries, Mayukh dropped the bombshell.

'I was thinking Sudha, Aadi and I could come down for a visit next weekend.'

There was silence at the other end, and Mayukh realized just how surprised his parents were at this sudden plan. His mother asked, hesitation apparent in her voice, 'Do you have a meeting here or something?'

'No, Ma, I just thought we haven't met in some time... I wanted to see you and also let Aadi spend some time with you.'

No vague promises of being there soon, no rationalizing about not being able to get time off from work. That was not how the NPV of Happiness worked, did it?

He then reconnected with two more old friends, one of whom had been his partner in crime when they had started a college newspaper. Well, more of a gossip magazine. Mayukh had soon got bored of the administrative aspects and they had got into too much trouble with the professors, but he had loved writing and seeing his name in print. That chat brought back a lot of good memories.

He booked the tickets for the trip to see his parents and called Sudha to just say hello. He had nothing specific to say, but then didn't the Cubicle Manifesto teach him that sometimes we do things the best when we have no specific agenda at all? Sudha was thrilled to hear about the upcoming trip over the weekend. She had been nagging Mayukh to make time to visit his parents for a long period, but with all the changes she had seen in her husband recently she was not really surprised to hear that he had already planned a trip. She wished him luck for his presentation in the afternoon.

Mayukh stole a glance at You Corp's stock before he left for the meeting, and saw that it was on a steep upward climb. That gave him the added confidence that no matter what happened in the meeting, it was but one factor that determined You Corp's fortunes.

When Mayukh entered the room, he saw Anupam standing there.

'Good luck.'

Mayukh thanked him politely, but knew that he had pretty much done everything he could to sabotage his chances. His email to the MD was meant to absolve himself of any responsibility if the project failed, and put the blame squarely on Mayukh's shoulders. Despite all that, Mayukh realized that he was not nervous. He had done everything he could, and knew that his team was counting on him, so he was not going to let them down. The meeting itself was much shorter than Mayukh had anticipated. After just one hour, the Managing Director said that he had seen quite enough. He had seemed very enthused during the presentation, asking a number of questions and strangely enough to Mayukh, not just about the ideas, but also how the team had conceived them. Mayukh answered truthfully

– that they were the result of the insights gained over a cup of latte and a chance re-connect with an old friend. He also brought his entire team in since he wanted them to be there when the fate of their project was decided. The Managing Director had nodded along, but his expression was inscrutable, so Mayukh didn't really know if the project would get the go-ahead or not.

When he came back to his cubicle, his team gathered around him in anticipation. But Mayukh was confident, and told them reassuringly that they had done their best and the rest was up to the company.

'I am really proud of you all. And no matter what happens, we will go out to celebrate in the evening,' he said.

An hour later, Mayukh was summoned to his boss's office and he could see him smiling broadly. Anupam had been called too, and as they entered the room, he whispered to Mayukh.

'Look, you gave it your best shot. So if it doesn't work out, don't sweat it.'

Mayukh smiled and his reply caught Anupam offguard.

'Anupam, I'm not stressed at all. It's just one meeting, about one project in one job. There are lots of other things in my life I am happy about, so it actually doesn't stress me at all.'

The Managing Director shook Mayukh's hand and congratulated him for the fantastic job he had done. He also told him that there was one thing which impressed him more than anything else – the whole feel of the place. He had been observing the team for the last few days, and had noticed several things – how energized the team was, how they seemed to work in harmony and how they all managed to keep their cool and balance despite working on a tough project. After hearing about how they had got some of their ideas, he had been even more impressed.

Mayukh was overwhelmed with the response. He had not really thought of success in the meeting going beyond salvaging the project and his career. But the experiences of the past few days seemed to have transformed not just how he approached work, but the results he was able to deliver.

'You know, Mayukh, we inject so much stress into our work that it often paralyses people. In my own career, I've found that I do best when I am actually enjoying work, not when I am terrified about what may happen if I fail. I am so glad your team not only pulled together and delivered, but also had fun doing it. Even if a few teams act like this, we could create a revolution in the whole work culture.'

Mayukh was stumped. He had never thought, or imagined, that he was bringing about any revolution, of any sort. He had just taken one small step at a time, and the whole catalyst had been the virus that had landed in his inbox. He figured that he would not be improving his career prospects by talking about a virus called the Cubicle Manifesto or a company called You Corp, so he settled for thanking the Managing Director.

He then called his team and gave them the good news. There was a collective whoop as they realized that all their hard work was indeed going to pay off. Then Mayukh called Sudha with the great news and told her that he might be a bit late as he was going out to celebrate with his team.

Mayukh's team were all pretty drunk, and Anupam looked like he had downed one too many as well. Mayukh laughed and joked around with them, but went slow with his drink. None of them really believed that their project had come this far, and Mayukh was genuinely embarrassed when one of his colleagues started raising toasts to him.

Tipsy as he was, Anupam tried to avoid Mayukh and when he was confronted by him, all he could manage was a sheepish look.

'Look, I didn't think we would…'

Mayukh didn't want to rub it in, so he gave Anupam a pat on his back, and said, 'Look, Anupam, I know you had given up on the project, and honestly, the way things looked a week ago, I couldn't blame you. But now we need to work together to get this project ready for marketing. What do you say?'

Anupam raised a toast to him in response, and they were soon joined by Mayukh's boss, who shook his hand and said, 'You had me worried for a while.'

'Worried? Why?'

His boss smiled. 'I was so sure you were going to quit.'

He then started reeling off a list of examples of behaviour that made him sure that Mayukh was on his way out. Leaving for home early, taking time off in the middle of an office day, blocking time on his calendar for 'connecting' when he didn't want any meetings or calls, and finally, not even looking stressed – despite the pressures of the project.

A funny thought struck Mayukh. Did one actually do better at work when one didn't try too hard, or worry too much? Was that part of the shift in mindset that would free someone from Cubicle Tyranny?

His boss then outlined several ideas that he had based on what he had observed Mayukh doing with his team. There would be no more meetings set up after six in the evening, teams would be encouraged to have a time slot every week when they got out of their cubicles and into the real marketplace to seek inspiration and ideas, and he would personally stop sending emails after work unless it was an emergency, and so on.

Mayukh smiled as he realized that his boss had picked up on at least some of the tips the virus had given him, and that it had taken a virus to hijack his laptop, and his life, to get him to realize what the Cubicle Manifesto provided.

It gave a person perspective.

Perhaps that was the biggest lesson Mayukh had learnt from the Cubicle Manifesto virus. The ability to keep the bigger picture in mind, and also to be able to do justice to all the facets of one's life instead of just obsessing about work and success.

He wondered if the virus had been right about Cubicle Tyranny after all. It was not the cubicle that imposed anything on anyone – the cubicle was a mere piece of furniture. The tyranny came from one's own mind, and how one became conditioned in one's approach to life after years of cubicle dwelling.

Now he realized that the Cubicle Manifesto could lead to a revolution, not a bloody insurrection. It was a revolution brought about by a series of small but important steps. Not one heralded by bloodthirsty mobs, but every individual taking responsibility for You Corp and inspiring others by quiet example instead of rabble-rousing speeches. As far as revolutions and overthrowing of tyrannies went, it was as peaceful and self-directed as it could be.

Mayukh's boss saw his pensive smile and asked him what other changes he had planned for his team. Mayukh said that he first wanted to ensure that he and his team could keep working the way they had been, on a day-to-day basis.

Just then his BlackBerry beeped, despite the fact that he had turned it off. Mayukh guessed it was his friendly neighbourhood virus at work. The message read:

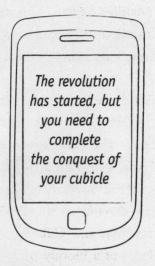

The revolution has started, but you need to complete the conquest of your cubicle

Mayukh wondered what that meant, but there were no more messages and his BlackBerry turned off on its own.

After a few more minutes, Mayukh excused himself and left for home, where he would celebrate his success with the biggest stakeholders of You Corp – his family.

SUSTAINING AND SPREADING THE MANIFESTO

'The only way to support a revolution is to make your own.'

ABBIE HOFFMAN

A week had passed since the meeting with the Managing Director, and Mayukh was in full flow as far as his new routine went. He ran almost every day, he took breaks during the day, went out with his team once a week in search of new ideas and, most importantly, he managed to give the time and attention to his family that they needed and expected.

His work continued to progress much better than it had ever before, and his cubicle was now almost as visibly transformed as his life.

Other than the work-related charts and files, personal photos and books, several other things important to the running of You Corp now adorned his cubicle. His vacation planner now ran into several sheets. This was to be the big European vacation he had promised his wife more than once over the last few years, but never really got around to actually creating time for. Now that he fully understood what the NPV of Happiness meant, he had slotted it in between some key milestones on his big project.

Mayukh realized that both his own liberation from Cubicle Tyranny and whether anyone else in his team maintained the momentum they had gained, would be tested in the week to come. That was because he would be on vacation and away from his cubicle as well as his team for more than a week.

He wondered what he would find when he came back.

The vacation was perhaps the most memorable one Mayukh had ever taken. He and his family had a wonderful time, visiting Italy and France, where he indulged in history and food, Sudha in art and shopping, and Aadi had a whale of a time at Disneyland. There was something for everyone, and while he had come closer to his family, thanks to the Cubicle Manifesto virus, this was definitely the icing on the cake.

On their flight back, it struck Mayukh that it had been more than a week since he had stepped into his office, and also more than a week since he had heard from the virus. He had not carried his laptop with him, and while he had carried his BlackBerry, he had not even turned it on. A month earlier, he would have panicked at the thought of not being in touch with his work on a daily basis, but with all that he had learnt from the Cubicle Manifesto, it now seemed to come naturally to him.

However, when he walked into the office the next day, he felt nervous. He couldn't really explain why...perhaps it had to do with the fact that he had no idea if, after such a break, he could sustain the way he had been working. One thing he was counting on was that the virus would be there to guide him, as it had in the weeks gone by. Without realizing it, he was beginning to miss it and its one-liners.

When he booted up his laptop he half-expected to see a welcome message from the virus, but there was nothing. He then clicked on his calendar, but all the entries the virus had put in it to help him follow its directions were gone. There was no early-morning slot for exercise, no brief time-outs for connecting or attending to personal errands, no Friday-afternoon sessions with his team outside the office. And, of course, there was no stock-price graph for You Corp to help him monitor his progress.

All gone.

Mayukh felt a stab of panic as he realized just how much he had come to depend on the virus.

Before he could think about it much longer, his boss welcomed him back by giving him some urgent work to do, and he got right to it. Without the virus giving him hints or shutting off his laptop, he worked through lunch without realizing it. In the evening, he got into a call with a supplier and then finished off his remaining work, and then looked at his watch to see that it was seven. Without the virus freezing his laptop at six, and with the time away from his cubicle, he realized that he was finding it hard to get back into the habits he had established with the virus's help. The next morning he did manage to get up for his run, but in the afternoon when he got his wife's call, he realized that he had totally forgotten to send flowers to her parents on their anniversary. Why had the virus not kept the slots on his calendar the way they had been?

Within just a couple of days of being back, Mayukh realized just how much of a fool he had been when he had started harbouring grandiose notions about helping his team and others to rid themselves of Cubicle Tyranny. What was obvious was the fact that without the virus to help him along, he could not even get back into the habits he had established just a week ago. And it was showing with the rest of his team as well. He saw them skip lunch along with him, and when he forgot their first brainstorming outside the office he could see the look of resignation on their faces.

Mayukh tried to remember all that the Cubicle Manifesto virus had taught him, and started putting in a few calendar entries, but without its constant written reminders it was hard to stay disciplined, and only too easy to get caught up in some 'urgent' work.

He wanted to make things the way they had been, and hoped the virus would be back to help him. Without the virus, perhaps there was no way he was going to be fully free of Cubicle Tyranny.

Mayukh fumbled along for the next couple of days and began to get really angry at the virus. What business did it have to come into his life, show him what was possible and then disappear without a trace when he needed it the most? Had it all been a sick prank or joke that someone had played on him?

He was feeling really low when his laptop screen went white and a single line of black text appeared. Mayukh felt his pulse quicken as he realized the virus had not abandoned him after all. The line read:

To sustain your
revolution against
Cubicle Tyranny,
write down
YOUR Manifesto

Mayukh immediately realized what the virus was trying to tell him. He did not need the virus to tell him on a day-to-day basis what he needed to do. The virus had already showed him the broad ideas and principles he needed to embrace to free himself from Cubicle Tyranny. Now the ball was in his court. All he needed to do was write down his own manifesto to guide him. That way he would not need the virus to remind him. Also, he knew the power of putting something down in writing – it made for a more concrete commitment. He remembered how putting entries in his calendar for his exercise and personal time had led him to honour them much more than he had ever before.

So Mayukh took a pen and paper and started writing:

MY CUBICLE MANIFESTO

I **choose** not to be a slave to Cubicle Tyranny.

My primary employer is **You Corp** and I will do
    what is right for its stakeholders.

The NPV of Happiness means I will **act now** when
    it comes to You Corp.

My calendar is my tool, not my master, and I will
    prioritize **appointments for myself**.

To think out of the box, I will take myself and my
    people **out of the box**.

I will **cut off the leash of the blinking red light**
    when I leave my cubicle.

I will **connect** to remind myself of what I am and
    who I was outside my cubicle.

I will bring my **personality into my cubicle** to
    show who's in charge here.

As Mayukh wrote down the words, he felt a big burden lift off his shoulders. He now knew he no longer needed the Cubicle Manifesto virus. He had everything he needed in his head, and, now, on a piece of paper. He stuck the paper on one of his cubicle walls and was not fazed once when several of his colleagues stopped by to see the strange list. He saw his team look at it and smile knowingly, and with more than a tinge of relief, as they realized that Mayukh had no intention of abandoning all the things that had made their lives and work so much smoother.

Mayukh got back to work, and soon his professional and personal life were going as smoothly as they had been when he was receiving daily coaching by the Cubicle Manifesto virus.

Except that now he no longer needed the virus.

Several weeks passed by and Mayukh knew, without requiring a graph to tell him, that You Corp was doing just fine. Work was better than ever, his team members were happier and he was much closer to his family. In short, he had everything he could ever hope for.

However, he also realized that his boss and the Managing Director had been quite serious about applying his way of working more broadly. He received a request from the

Managing Director to hold an informal chat with some employees outside his immediate work group on the ideas he was trying to implement. He would have thought the HR Manager would object, but he came up to Mayukh and admitted that he now believed in what he was trying to do and wanted to help him. Whether that was because the HR Manager was now convinced of the fact that Mayukh's team was actually happier and performing better on the job, or if it was simply because the Managing Director had endorsed it, Mayukh did not know, nor did he ask.

Mayukh did have the chat, but he realized that what everyone wanted was something he just could not provide. Everyone, perhaps conditioned by years of looking at business and results through black and white metrics, wanted a magic formula that they could apply to their work. He knew that was not going to work. Every person worked for their own You Corp, which had its own stakeholders. A person who was not married or did not have kids would have very different stakeholders compared to him. Similarly, someone who lived with their parents would have their own needs. Every person also had their own personality to bring to their cubicles, and every person had their own kind of personal time they needed to make space for.

Mayukh realized that the only way to help anyone else be free of Cubicle Tyranny was not to try and offer them a ready-made solution. The trick was to help them understand the ideas behind the Cubicle Manifesto and let them ask themselves the hard questions of how its lessons could best fit into their lives.

The problem was that he had no way of doing that. He came back to his cubicle, ready to pack up and leave for the day, when he saw one last message from the Cubicle Manifesto virus. It was a new calendar entry, strangely enough set at ten at night – a time when he knew his son would be asleep and he and Sudha would usually watch TV before going to bed. It was a thirty-minute appointment, and the title simply read:

One last thing –
spread the
Manifesto in
your own way

He had no idea what that meant, but noticed that the calendar entry indicated that he needed his laptop for this appointment. He had not told Sudha about the virus, but since she had been one of the first to notice the changes in him and also one of the people most impacted by it, he told her about how he had learnt of some new ideas to manage his work and life. She was very supportive, and so that night after dinner he told her that he would spend half an hour working on a project that would help others learn some of those lessons.

That night at ten, as Sudha watched TV next to him, Mayukh booted up his laptop, wondering what the virus had in mind for his last gift. When his laptop came on, Mayukh saw that the word processor software filled the screen. So the virus wanted him to write something. But what could that be? And what could that have to do with spreading the Cubicle Manifesto's message in his own way? Then he noticed a line of words forming on the screen.

A book?

He then realized what the virus was trying to remind him of. His long-forgotten dream of being a writer. He had no idea if anybody would ever publish his book, or how far he would go towards writing it. Yet, he began, and, almost without thinking, the title suggested itself as he typed it.

The Cubicle Manifesto.

As his fingers hovered over the keyboard and he wondered how to begin, he smiled and then began typing.

Cubicle dwellers of the world unite...

Acknowledgements

The first and biggest vote of thanks goes to the biggest shareholders in my You Corp – my wife, Puja, and our son, Aaditya. I don't need a virus or a manifesto to keep me grounded or to tell me how important the NPV of Happiness is. Just seeing them every day reminds me of what is really important in life. Escaping the tyranny of one's cubicle above all requires having something to look forward to beyond work and, on that count, I feel like the luckiest man in the world to have such a wonderful family.

The 'founding partners' of my You Corp are no longer with me, but I'm sure they're up there, together again, looking down on what the son of theirs who since grade 5 had the crazy notion of being a writer is up to. My father, Maloy, who passed away recently, may not have had the benefit of a virus hijacking his computer, but his own revolution came from within, and, after publishing his first book at the age of 58, he went on to become a bestselling author. My mother, Sunanda, left me in 2001, but she was the one who really fed my writing bug by encouraging a precocious child who dreamt of being a writer.

Once again, I was delighted to work with the team at Random House, and the finished book you hold in your hands owes a lot to their inputs and efforts. A book may begin as an idea in the head of a writer, and sometimes writing it can be a solitary exercise, but bringing it to life as a finished product is truly a team effort.